CAJUN DICTIONARY

CAJUN DICTIONARY

A COLLECTION OF SOME COMMONLY USED WORDS & PHRASES BY THE PEOPLE OF SOUTH LOUISIANA.

James M. Sothern
Illustrations by Jerry Charpentier

INTRODUCTION

The way Cajuns speak english is perhaps the most unique and interesting ethnic dialect existing today in America. Until the last 20 years or so however, this jocular patois, spoken only in South Louisiana, generally went unnoticed except in areas within close proximity to southern Louisiana.

There are several reasons for the recent and widespread awareness of Cajun english outside the proximal area of Acadiana, as South Louisiana is frequently called. Increased tourism throughout the United States in the last few decades, the recent upsurge in cultural and ethnic awareness by the general public, and the rapid economic growth of South Louisiana, resulting in an influx of people from all over, are some of the major factors contributing to the extensive cognizance of the Acadian life style.

One of the most unique facets of Cajun english is the innate, built-in humor that is readily detectable when and where Cajuns gather. Although the words used (and missused) in Cajun english were brought about originally by a lack of formal education among some of the older constituents, many of the grammatically incorrect phrases and exclamations are purposely made and not spoken through ignorance.

This jovial and waggish attitude prevalent among Cajuns is deep rooted. The marshes, swamps and coastal waters of South Louisiana abound with fish and wildlife of great variety and abundance, so that the pioneer lifestyle persisted in Acadiana well into the twentieth century. Even today, Cajuns live close to nature, with fishing and hunting being the most popular forms of recreation, or livelyhood, for that matter. Deep down inside, Cajuns know that if times get too hard, they can always survive and have food on the table. Perhaps this is why there are so many happy people in Acadiana.

PREFACE TO THE SECOND EDITION

When the first edition of the Cajun Dictionary appeared in 1977 only 500 copies were printed as the book was originally designed as a gift item for the authors friends and business associates, hence the inexpensive and diminuitive construction. The demand soon became such that it was no longer possible to continue donating the book so that a charge covering distribution and printing costs was necessarily required.

Several thousand copies were sold when, upon the advice of friends and acquaintances involved in book sales, it was decided that a second edition should be prepared utilizing more illustrations and art work. This was accomplished with the fine artistry of Jerry Charpentier of Houma, who not only provided all the sketches contained within, but also assisted with the organization and layout of the second edition.

ACADIANA

The culture of South Louisiana is so different from that of the rest of the state that one is tempted to let the imagination run wild and suppose that a new state be formed from the southern part of Louisiana. The name of this new state would be Acadiana.

The boundaries of this new state would be from the Sabine River on the west to the Pearl River on the east. The southern boundary would, of course, be the Gulf of Mexico, out to 300 miles. The northern boundary would be a line through Baton Rouge just north of Tiger Stadium at L.S.U.

However, other areas adjacent to these boundary lines may want to be annexed such as the Port Authur, Texas area which has a high Cajun population, and parts of southern Mississippi around Biloxi which Cajuns like to visit.

The state capitol would be Lafayette, due to its central location. The state flower would be the azalea, and the state tree would be the moss-draped live oak. The state bird must certainly be the french duck or mallard. He is loyal to his mate, and is the wariest of all game birds but will become tame and friendly when treated with kindness. Both male and female have great pride and affection for their young ones. These are all traits cherished by the Cajun people.

The state flag would be a white banner divided into four squares by a golden cross. The Confederate battle flag would appear in the upper right corner and a fleur de lis in the lower left corner. In the upper left corner would be Evangeline's oak and a crayfish in the lower right corner.

These symbols on our new flag would represent the following:

The white banner - honesty and loyalty.

The gold cross - Christianity.

The Confederate battle flag - courage and love of liberty.

The evangeline oak - patience.

The fleur de lis - our French heritage.

The crayfish - love of good food and fellowship.

These also, are traits cherished by the Cajun people.

In addition, both French and English would be spoken by everyone and the state motto would be- *"Laisse les bons ton rouler"* - *"Let the good times roll"*. And finally, the state song would be *"Jolie Blon"*.

ISBN 0-9673487-0-6 5.95

Distributed By:
Bayou Printing & Graphics, Inc.
922 Sunset Avenue • Houma, Louisiana 70360
(985) 868-8273
www.bayouprinting.com

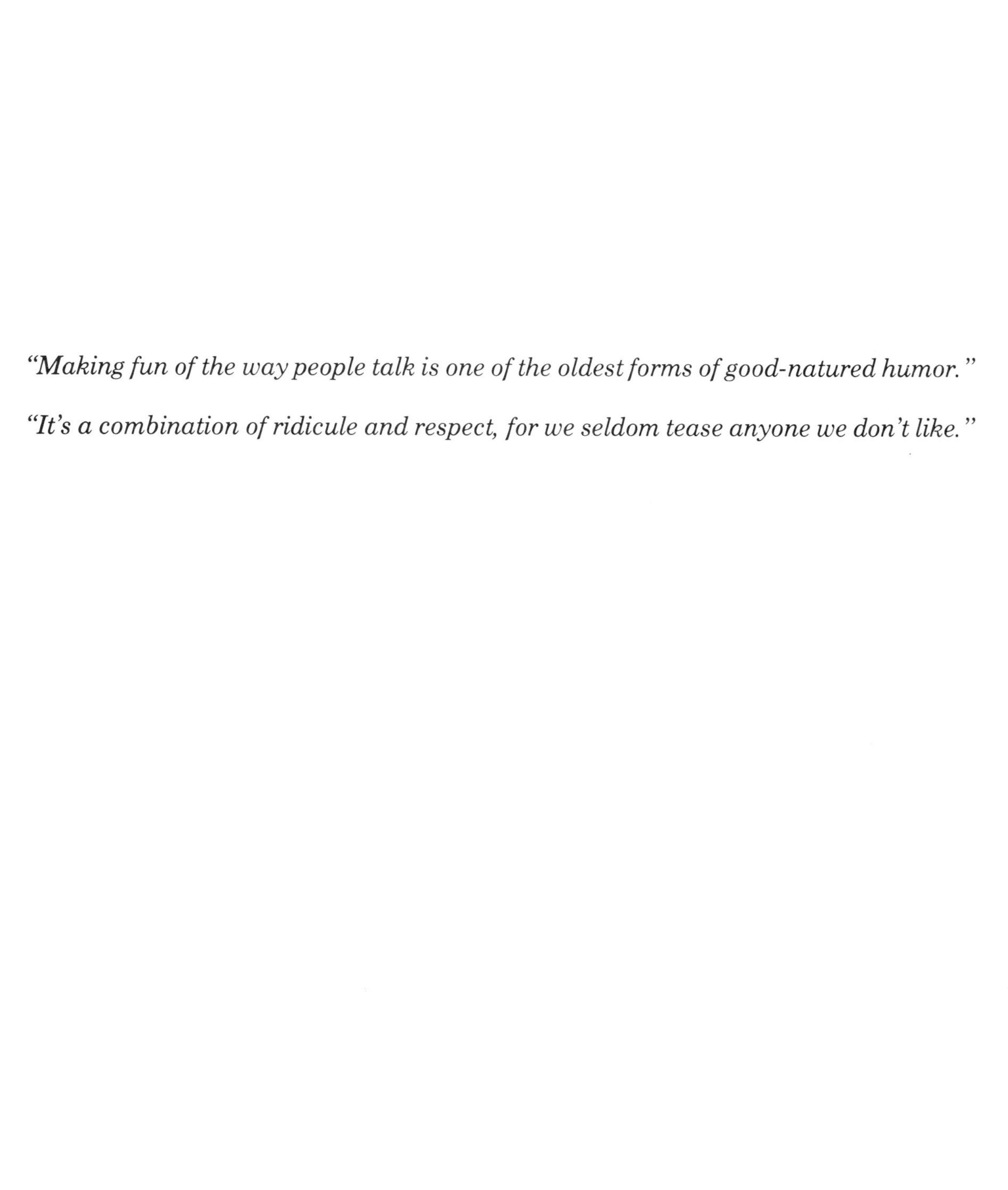

"Making fun of the way people talk is one of the oldest forms of good-natured humor."

"It's a combination of ridicule and respect, for we seldom tease anyone we don't like."

A

a, as in English, but also for emphasis with the negative or positive.
*"**A** no, you can't borrow my pirogue!"*

abdominal, detestable, horrible.
*"If you don get a hair cut you gone to look like de **abdominal** snowman."*

ablum, a collection of music on record.
*"I got a **ablum** by Charlie Pride at de store."*

adjutif, descriptive words usually repeated two or three times.
"His boat is big, big, but mine is fast, fast, fast!"

ag, the round reproductive body of birds or animals.
*"I like my gumbo wit turtle **ag.**"*

ah, I, the first person.
*"**Ah** like you."*

ak, the process of doing.
*"Why don you **ak** right."*

all, petroleum.
*"Check de **all** too, please."*

all patch, the oil industry.
This phrase is very common throughout the oil industry but has its origin in South Louisiana, although it is not known just how it first came into use. One version is that when the first drilling rigs began to arrive in South Louisiana, the term oilfield brought confusion to the Cajun people because in Acadiana a field or garden was always called a patch. One day an old Cajun went out to look for a job on a drilling rig near his farm. The driller and crew, all being from Texas, went into hysterics when the Cajun, clad in overalls and hip boots, went upon the rig floor and asked if he could have a job on the "**all patch**."

alma dillon, armadillo. (Also called elmer davis and ammarillo depending on what bayou you're on.)
"Ther's no more turtles, de **alma dillions** *dig up all de ags."*

ahm gon, I am going to.
*"Mamma can I go to de show? "***Ahm gon** *show you!"*

anh, a reply used when one does not understand or as an expression of surprise.
*"Oh, Telest, lan me ten dollars?" "***Anh***!"*

antan, a device for electronic reception.
"Check de **antan,** *de T.V.'s on de blank."*

any coast, the intracoastal canal.
"De tugs are so tick on de **any coast** *you got time to die before de bridge open."*

an you, a versatile reply meaning, you also.
*"You sure got a big nose" - "***an you***!"*

arrow pleen, airplane
"Ah don lak to fly in dem big jat **arrow pleen***."*

arry, each, all, every.
*"***Arry** *body likes jambalaya."*

arryting, everything
*"***Arryting** *is so high today."*

avery, variation of arry, used mostly in southwest Louisiana.
*"***Averyone** *is invited."*

aw, an expression of doubt or amazement.
*"Ah caught a 30 lb. green trout last week" - "***Aw***"*

ax, ask
*"***Ax** *him if he wants some more gumbo."*

B

bad, a piece of furniture used for sleeping.
"He's sick in de **bad***."*

bag dare, in the rear, away from civilization, in back of.
"He went **bag dare** *in de swamp."*

ball, to boil
"Ya'll come over tonight, we gonna **ball** *some crawfish!"*

ban, the Cajun pronunciation of the French **bien** meaning; well, O.K., alright, etc. Usually used together with the English as an affirmative reply.
O.K., **ban***, alright, I'll see you later."*

Here come dat pest orestile, call him an tell him dat we don got no swimps - but close de hatch first.

bat, to wash or bathe
"Go take a **bat***, you stink!"*

Boo-dree-ox, how Rednecks & Yankees pronounce Boudreaux.

booray, a card game played in Acadiana. Also, to lose or go broke.
"You gonna **booray** *if you try dat hand."*

boon, a part of the skeletal structure.
"He fell out de rig and broke his leg **boon***."*

bruzzer, brother
"Go get you **bruzzer** *an ya'll come eat."*

burtday, birthday
"When's you **burtday***?"*

bye, bayou
"Get out dat pirogue, you gonna drown in dat **bye***!"*

byok, an offensive or overbearing person.
"Dats all a bunch of **byoks** *at de license bureau."*

C

cam, tranquil, calm
"De fish should bite, de waters **cam***."*

cane, cannot
"Ah **cane** *go to de dance."*

cause, the price paid to aquire something.
"How much does dat **cause***?"*

car porch, a roof extension used for parking cars (car port)
"My **car porch** *leaks arrytime it rains."*

cher pacan, a versatile exclamation used to evoke ridicule, doubt, or amazement.
*"***Cher pacan***! You saw how she was dress - high heel shoe and pink sock!"*

chester freeze, ice chest (not widely used - fortunately)
"The beer's in de **chester freeze***."*

chew, from the French slang meaning rear end or behind. In Cajun dialect, it may also mean the whole person especially if he is undesirable.
"Get you **chew** *off my boat."*

chew rouge, irritated, provoked. Translated literally, a red rear end.
"Dat fellow gives me de **chew rouge***."*

chiren, infants or young ones
"Call de **chiren***, Popeye's on T.V."*

chock a block, very abundant, packed.
"De lake is **chock a block** *wit duck."*

chockay, incoherently drunk.
"You gone to get **chockay** *wit dat cheap wine!"*

chu chut, a general purpose substitute for naming any small object or device.
"De motor wont run wit out dat little **chu chut** *dere."*

chune, to tune a musical instrument or engine.
"Dat motor needs a **chune***-up."*

coil, to telephone to
*"***Coil** *me later, my old man's home from offshore."*

congo, cotton-mouth moccasin (probably African in origin)
"Watch out for de **congo** *in de duck blind."*

Come see quick. Alphonse, dey got a new all patch in de bayou!

conja, a conjurer or any object used to induce voodoo, also **conjo**.
"Dat old woman is a **conja***."*

coo, a very enthusiastic expression of amazement.
*"***Coo***! Look at de size of dem shrimp!"*

coon ice, the phonetic pronunciation of what a Texan calls a Cajun.

cooyon, stupid, dumb, also an educated fool.
"If dem **cooyon** *engineers don stop digging canals all over, we gonna all flood."*

crackaboon, a chiropractor
"De **crackaboon** *is cheaper den de doctor."*

crease-moose, Christmas
"What Santa Clause brought you for **crease-moose***?"*

D

d, always used in place of "th", i.e. dem people, de car, dose apples, etc.
"All **dough dis** *is your boat,* **dat** *is my motor."*

deen ween, didn't win
"I went to bingo last night, but ah **deen ween.***"*

do do, to sleep (from the French dormir)
"It's time to make **do do***, I got to get up at five tomorrow."*

dubba, twofold
"I got **dubba** *my money back on dat deal."*

dumata, a red pulpy garden vegetable
"My favorite vegetable is a **dumata.***"*

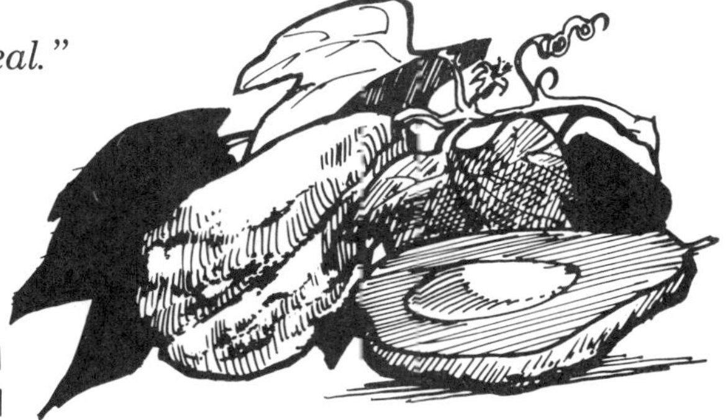

E

each, irritation of the skin
"I **each** *all over."*

een, within, inclusion
"He's all de time **een** *trouble."*

een dare, within
"Dare's a big coon **een dare***."*

Emmet N. Domangue, the ability of the state to exappropriate property with compensation. (eminent domain)
"You can't stop de new highway from crossing you land. Dey gonna take it anyway with **Emmet N. Domangue***."*

eveling, afternoon evening
"I don drink beer until in de **eveling***."*

enemy, injection of liquid into rectum
"If you eat too much cheese, you'll have to have a **enemy***."*

F

fay dodo, a dance or party
Editor's Note: fay dodo literally means "go to sleep" in Cajun dialect. In time past, many Cajun parents could not afford a baby sitter, so when there was a dance, the children were brought along but were made to "fay dodo" so that their parents could enjoy the evening.
"De last time we went to a **fay dodo** *all you did was dance with T-Harry's wife!"*

Fee Folay, a mysterious object usually in the form of a flaming ball, common in Cajun legend and folklore. (From the French, feu folie, meaning foolish fire.)
"You better come inside de **Fee Folay** *gonna get you."*

fonchock, origin unknown, but is used to describe a sly-looking person or a smart aleck. (Possibly from the French, chafouin)
"I wouldn't vote for him, he's too **fonchock***."*

fooyay, to meddle, a foolish act
"Ah told you not to **fooyay** *with Alcide's tool box."*

four michael, formica
"Honey, if we catch planty of shrimp dis season, can I have some **four michael** *on my kitchen cabinets."*

fratch, a peculiar expression rather recent in use. An inconvenience, mishap, breakdown, etc.
"Dat was a brand noo car and first time I drove it to town - **fratch***! in de tunnel."*

G

ga, to look, look at (Derived from the French word, regarder - to look at.)
*"***Ga***, here come Octave wit his new gilfran!"*

gaga, someone prone to be too inquisitive, (literally look, look)
"Arrytime we pass in front of her house dat **gaga** *is rocking on de porch."*

galee, an expression used to denote surprise or astonishment. (Perhaps from the English, golly, or vice-versa.)
*"***Galee***, it's you dat was dressed up like dat for Mardi Gras!"*

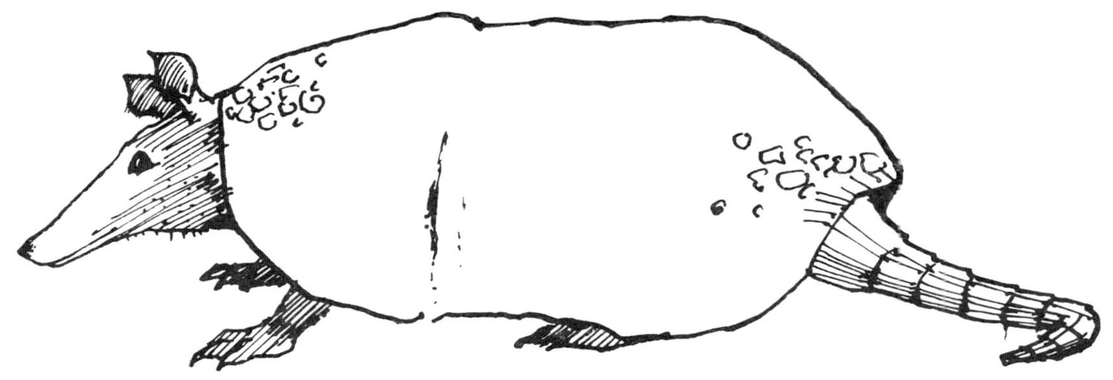

goat rocks, how Rednecks & Yankees pronounce **Gautreaux.**

gang warden, a wildlife agent
"Throw de pooldoos° in de marsh here come de **gang warden***!"*
°**pooldoo,** a coot (French poule d'eau)

gogo, a slang expression for making love
"My husband never wants to go anywhere, all he ever thinks about is gumbo, **gogo***, and dodo."*

gou gut, (gou as in you, gut as in put) a slovenly stupid person
"Don't stand dere lak a **gou gut,** *hand me de saw."*

gree gree, (French gris, meaning gray, origin unknown, possibly African) any object or contrivance used to conjure harm or evil to the recipient.
"If dat new guy don't stop foolin wit ma girl, ahm gon put a **gree gree** *on him."*

guff, large body of water, Gulf of Mexico.
"Let's go to Grand Island, de **guff** *is cam."*

H

had, the upper part of the body, also the brain.
"You might as well get it into you **had,** *you can't go to dat trashy place."*

hafass, low grade, half hearted effort, inferior
"Dat's a **hafass** *job if I ever saw one."*

hairline, a major thoroughfare in New Orleans (Airline)
"Dey had a bad wreck on de **hairline***."*

Halo Statue, a reply over the telephone, when the answering party is familiar

Harry, profuse amount of hair
"De music is alright, but de band's too **harry**.*"*

hayacall, used to denote any object or creature for which the name is unknown
"Dat **hayacall** *jumped out de tree and ate him in de show."*

Hewtin, Houston, Texas
"I always wanted to go to **Hewtin**, *but I'm afraid to cross all dem mountains."*

hormel, substance formed in Endocrine glands
"Dem **hormel** *pills make all dem women crazy."*

hose-pipe, water hose (strangely, this term is also common in England)
"Pick up de **hose-pipe** *befo you cut de grasses."*

I

I, seldom pronounced as such. In Cajun dialect: I is pronounced as ah, but pronounced as e when preceeding a consonant. Ex. in pronounced as een.

if, used often as a strong affirmative reply
"You lak to dance?" - **"If!"**

Ion, a common metal, also to press clothes
"Ion *you own dress, lazy."*

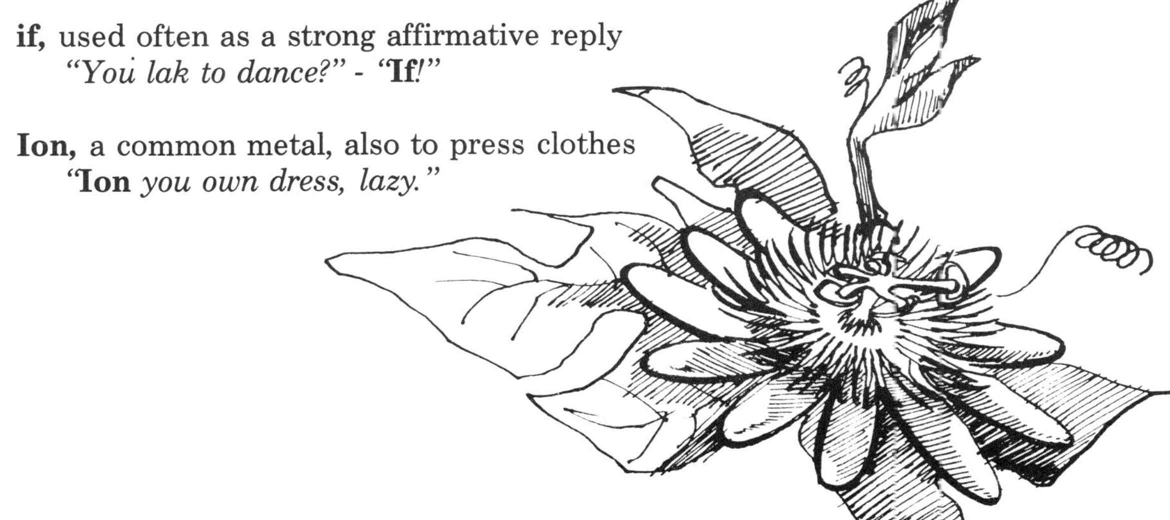

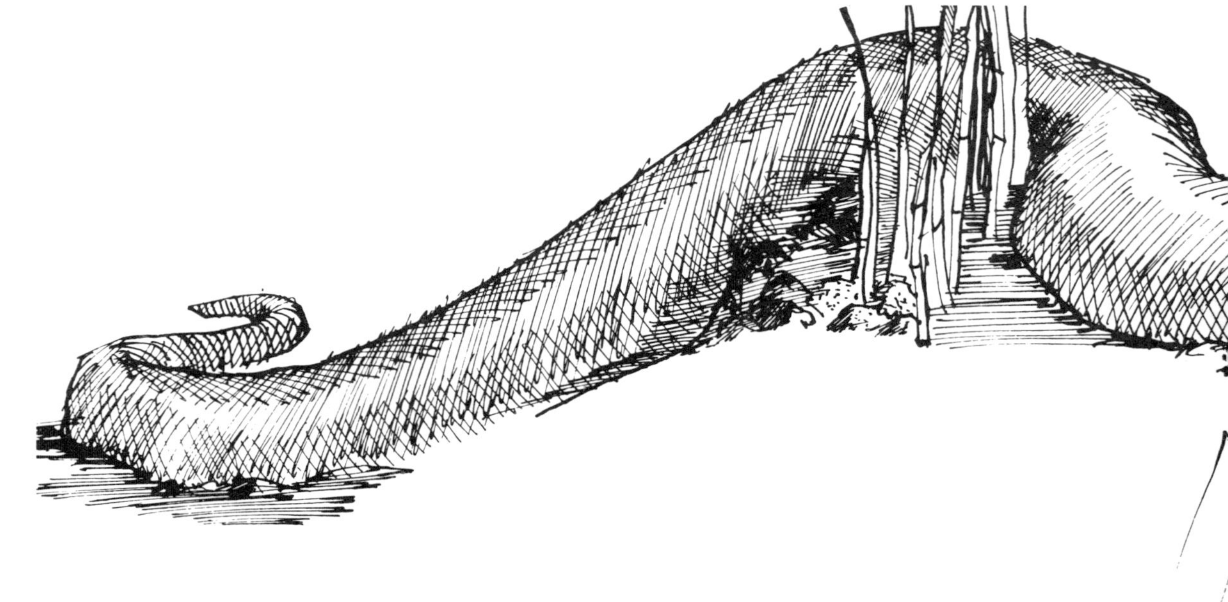

J

jaws, a glass container

"Tante (Aunt) Cecile sent us 12 **jaws** *of fig preserves."*

Jaypan, Japanese

"All dem **Jaypan** *radios is trash."*

joint, large, monstrous

"Man, dat Superdome is a **joint** *place."*

juga keen, sugar cane

"Arry time dey spray de **juga keen** *it kills all de doves."*

junya, a young boy, junior

"Oh, **Junya***, quit teasing you sister."*

K

kang, a metal container
"Pop me another **kang** *of Bud, please."*

kritspee, crispy
"We out of bread, eat de rice **kritspee**."

L

lak, to show affection
"Ah **lak** *her but she don* **lak** *me."*

launch, noon meal
"He was fired from NASA because he taut a **launch** *pad was where you went to eat."*

leaf, to go away, depart
"**Leaf** *me alone!"*

loan motor, a device for cutting grass
"With all dis rain de grasses is too high for de **loan motor**."

loopey long, The Huey P. Long Bridge
Ah don like to go to New Orleans de **loopey long** *is too narrow."*

M

ma, possessive adjective
"**Ma** *feet hurt!"*

marry, happy, gay
"**Marry** *crease-moose"*

may, but, well (from the French - mais)
"**May**, *ah taut you brought de bait."*

me, same as in English but frequently used with I
"I'm gone to town, **me**."

metry, a system of measurement
"Why we gotta have dat **metry** *system, arrybody knows dat 2 pints equals 1 quart, 4 quarts equals 1 gallon, and may, 5 gallons equals a 5 gallon kang."*

moodee, cursed, foul, no good
"Dat **moodee** *loan motor never starts until you crank you arm off."*

mystery, action that annoys (mischief)
"Dat boy is all de time full of **mystery**."

N

Nannan, god mother
"I wish ma **nannan** *was rich lak you* **nannan**."

neutral, nutria (also called nunya, muriel, nutta. etc.)
Dem **neutrals** *will bite you if you not careful."*

nonk, uncle
You nose is big like **Nonk** *Justin."*

nort, north
"All de crabs is gone up **nort**."

nuttin, nothing
"**Nuttin** *went right today."*

O

ohm, house, home
"It's time for you to go **ohm***."*

oil, always, all
"Ever since he went to work in de all patch he's **oil** *de time drunk."*

oovkang, can opener (from French ouvrir to open and kang (can)
"You hardly see dem **oovkangs** *anymore since day come out wit dem pop a tops."*

ovadaddy, over there, away from
"He's way **ovadaddy** *across de lake."*

Quit sucking dem heads cochon, and peel you little girl some crawfish.

P

palometta, a tan horse with golden tail and mame
"Dey had a lotta **palomettas** *at de AG fair."*

paunch, to poke, hit
"Shut up or I'm gonna **paunch** *you."*

peeve, concrete road
"Dey need to **peeve** *dis road to get rid of de holes."*

pansil, implement used for writing
"Don't run wit dat **pansil** *in you mouth!"*

pass by, to go into, to stop
"On you way home **pass by** *de store and pick up some boudin."*
(**boudin,** cajun sausage)

plareen, candy made from sugar and pecans
"He eats too may **plareens** *dats why he ain't got no teeth."*

plarie, marsh
"Every duck season he live in de **plarie**.*"*

pleece, deputy, law officer
"Keep you dog in you yard or I'm gonna call the **pleece**.*"*

pleet, plate
"De **pleet** *launch is good at Annie's."*

plerch, edible freshwater fish
"Green trout an **plerch** *is my favorite fishes."*

pooyie, distasteful, offensive
*"You smelled dat perfume she has on." "***Pooyie**!*"*

prospect, male gland at base of urethra
"Nonk Harry had trouble wit his **prospect** *gland."*

Q

No Q in Cajun Alphabet.

You de first labatory retriever ah seen dats afraid of ducks.

R

rad, Crimson, scarlet, also to blush
"His face turn **rad** *when she left wit dat other guy."*

ranch, to wash off
"Always use cistern water to **ranch** *the dishes."*

rat cheer, in front of, before you
"**Rat cheer** *is where we caught all dem trouts."*

roday, to run around, on the go
Avery time her old man goes offshore all she does is **roday**."

Rob E. Chocks, how Rednecks & Yankees pronounce Robichaux.

Roogaroo, a kind of supernatural creature but may also mean to make mischief.
(probably originated from the French word for werewolf - loupgarou)
May, I couldn't sleep at all, he made de **roogaroo** *all night."*

S

s, seldom used with the plural often with the singular
"Ah lak crab, shrimps and oyster."

salse, a seasoned preparation usually containing tomatoes, onions, garlic, etc.
"Clovis is cleaning de turtles, you can start wit de **salse**."

seem, alike, identical
"All dem politicians is de **seem**."

How come de gang wardens don't arrest dat spray pleen? He done kill 5 time de limit!

severe, land surveyor
"Ah'm gone see de **severe,** *he built dat fence across ma propitty."*

sha, dear, precious (from the French cher)
"Oh **sha**, *you want to dance."*

shad, small building
"Daddy you better go see what bruzzer is doin in de **shad**."

shaws, thing, matter, affair, also a verb - to activate, to do something (French-chose)
"No telling what kind of **shaws** *day gonna find on Mars."*

she, used with nouns to denote gender
"Ma car, **she** *is broke."*

shoepick, a large fresh water fish found mostly in swamps and bayous: cypress trout.
"Crawfish is de best bait for **shoepicks**."

slug ranch, a special tool for changing automobile tires.
"Ah had a flat in de middle of Main Street and no **slug ranch** *in de trunk."*

swimps, edible crustacean common in South Louisiana
"Don forget de **swimps** *fo de gumbo tomorrow."*

T

T, small, petite, little; also used as a nickname when affixed with surname. T-Boy, T-Harry, T-Cat, etc.
"He don lak for you to call him **T**-*Norman since he moved to de city."*

tan, the number ten
"**Tan** *dollars is too high for khaki pants."*

tanks, to express gratitude
"**Tanks** *for letting me use you duck blind.*"

teeree, the number 3 (roll the "r")
"All ah got left is **teeree** *dollars."*

teet, dentition
"He laughed so hard his **teet** *fell in de aisle."*

Texyan, what a Cajun calls someone from Texas, usually accompanied by moodee.
"Dem moodee **texyans** *all de time make fun of us."*

tie loose, to untie
"**Tie loose** *de boat!*"

tied, exhausted, weary, impatient
"Ah'm **tied** *of dat job."*

tink, thought, thinking, concept
"What you **tink**, *ah'm crazy."*

true, in one end, out the other
"He fell **true** *de roof."*

trow, to hurl or propel, also to put
"**Trow** *it in second gear or you gonna get stuck.*"

tunda, the loud noise which accompanies lightning or the lightning bolt.
"Don stand under dat tree, you will be hit by de **tunda**."

tursty, craving drink
"Let's stop at de Bon Ton Roule, ah'm **tursty**."

twat, person or thing of a derogatory nature, also rear end or butt
"Tell dat little **twat** *to go home."*

U

udder, another person or thing
"A no, it was dat **udder** *guy what slapped you."*

umpie, referee
"De **umpie** *was for dem, dats why we lost."*

V

vary, extremely
"Ah am **vary** *hungry."*

very close, swollen veins (varicose)
"If dem women would walk in de marsh lak dey used to, dey wouldn't have dem **very close** *vein!"*

violet, raging, disorderly, violent.
"When ah told him he pay too much for dat boat, he got **violet***."*

vote, unit of electromotive force
"It takes a 24 **vote** *battery to crank dat moodee machine."*

W

warse, stinging insect
"He's mean lak a **warse***."*

weakling, to move from side to side
"Stop **weakling** *T-Boy, de Preese is looking at you."*

wone, to gain or succeed
"Ah **wone** *eight dollars playing booray."*

X

X-rated, to examine by means of X-ray
"You better go have you had **X-rated***!"*

Dare is no more wine een dare, T-Noon got chockayed and left de bottle in de duck blind.

Y

yallo, bright color like that of lemon
*"Dat **yallo** dress she had on for de wedding was tacky."*

year, the organ of hearing
*"Dat fonchock had a ring on his **year**."*

yestitty, the day preceeding
*"Ah know **yestitty** was you burtday, but today you lak de rest of us."*

RICE

Dem neutrals is getting so fonchock and nervy, ah gone have to switch to a steel pirogue!

zinc, a basin in a kitchen
"Don wash you hands in de **zinc***."*